D1593257

# TRAVELLING IN THE FAMILY

*Edited by Thomas Colchie*
*and Mark Strand*

*with additional translations*
*by Elizabeth Bishop*
*and Gregory Rabassa*

# TRAVELLING IN THE FAMILY

*Selected Poems*

## CARLOS DRUMMOND DE ANDRADE

RANDOM HOUSE

NEW YORK

Some of the translations by Thomas Colchie originally appeared in the following publications: *The New York Review of Books, Paris Review* and *Review: Latin American Literature and Arts.* "To a Hotel Scheduled for Demolition" first appeared in *The Hudson Review.* Copyright © 1972, 1976, 1985 by Thomas Colchie.

Grateful ackowledgment is made to the following for permission to reprint previously published translations by Mark Strand and Elizabeth Bishop: "Looking for Poetry" and "Story of the Dress," translated by Mark Strand, originally appeared in *Antaeus.* "Boy Crying in the Night," translated by Mark Strand, originally appeared in *The Antioch Review,* Volume 34, Number 4, 1976. "The Dirty Hand," translated by Mark Strand, originally appeared in *Reasons for Moving,* copyright © 1968 by Mark Strand, and is reprinted with the permission of Atheneum Publishers, Inc. "Seven-Sided Poem," "Infancy," "In the Middle of the Road," "Don't Kill Yourself, "Travelling in the Family," "Family Portrait" and "The Table," translated by Elizabeth Bishop, appeared in *Elizabeth Bishop: The Complete Poems 1927–1979,* copyright © 1983 by Alice Helen Methfessel, copyright © 1969 by Elizabeth Bishop, and are reprinted by permission of Farrar, Straus and Giroux, Inc. "Souvenir of the Ancient World" and "Quadrille," translated by Mark Strand, first appeared in *Grilled Flowers.* "Motionless Faces," "Residue," "Song of the Phantom Girl of Belo Horizonte," "Song for a Young Girl's Album" and "Death in a Plane," translated by Mark Strand, first appeared in *The New Yorker,* copyright © 1976 by The New Yorker Magazine, Inc. "An Ox Looks at Man," "The Onset of Love," "In the Golden Age" and "Ballad of Love Through the Ages," translated by Mark Strand, first appeared in *The New Yorker,* copyright © 1980, 1981, 1982, 1983 by Mark Strand. "The Dead in Frock Coats" and "The Elephant," translated by Mark Strand, originally appeared in *Ploughshares,* 1975. "Interpretation of December," translated by Mark Strand, first appeared in *Porch.* "Seven-Sided Poem," "Dawn," "Don't Kill Yourself" and "José," translated by Mark Strand first appeared in *Seneca Review.*

Library of Congress Cataloging-in-Publication Data

Andrade, Carlos Drummond de, 1902–
Travelling in the family.

1. Andrade, Carlos Drummond de, 1902– —Translations, English. I. Colchie, Thomas. II. Title.
PQ9697.A7185A24   1986      869.1        86-10009
ISBN 0-394-74751-8 (pbk.)

*Manufactured in the United States of America*

2 4 6 8 9 7 5 3

FIRST EDITION

*Book design by Carole Lowenstein*

# *Acknowledgments*

I would like to express my appreciation to the Ingram Merrill Foundation for their generous support, and to Farrar, Straus & Giroux for their permission to reprint the late Elizabeth Bishop's translations of Carlos Drummond de Andrade, which were the inspiration for this volume. I also want to acknowledge my debt to Mark Strand for translating from poetry into poetry so many "impossible" Drummond poems. And finally, my thanks to Gregory Rabassa for his version of "Supposed Existence," which points to the many aspects of the later Drummond that also deserve translation.

T. C.

# Contents

# *Introduction*

Brazil is often regarded by North Americans as an exotic parenthesis to Latin America—a tropical "aside," though subcontinental in size. Even the Portuguese language of its more than 140 million inhabitants is viewed parenthetically: as that *other* language which is *not* Spanish. Consequently, Brazil has remained until quite recently Latin America's best-kept secret.

The same may be said of Brazilian poetry. If asked to name some Latin American poets, even a reader who can readily cite such writers as Cesar Vallejo from Peru, Pablo Neruda from Chile, or Octavio Paz from Mexico is unlikely to have heard of Mário or Oswald de Andrade, Manuel Bandeira or João Cabral de Melo Neto from Brazil.

This book attempts to redress the balance by presenting a selection of the century's finest and most accessible poet writing in the Portuguese language. It may seem strange to the North American reader to hear greatness and accessibility attributed to the same poet. Rarely have the two coincided in our poetry, at least since Whitman. In Latin America, two of the greatest modern poets—the Chilean Pablo Neruda and the Brazilian Carlos Drummond de Andrade—have also been tremendously popular.

No modern poet—not even Neruda—has managed to construct so intimate a rapport with his reader as Carlos Drummond de Andrade. Neruda is an intensely social poet: public, epic, even in matters as personal as love. Carlos Drummond is quieter, more lyrical and self-effacing, tenaciously private even while sharing Neruda's social concerns. Where they differ is in register. Neruda speaks to, sings of the common man. He is the great popular voice in modern Latin American poetry, as anyone who heard him read will attest. Drummond, on the other hand, represents the poet as listener: he would hear the common man and personify him in his verse. This effort spans the sixty-odd years of Drummond's poetic output and attains its great realization in the "proletariat biographies" such as "The Disappearance of Luisa Porto" and "Story of the Dress," but above all in "Song for That Man of the People Charlie Chaplin."

The figure of "Carlitos," as Chaplin was known in Brazil, offers perhaps the greatest single key to Drummond's poetics: the consummate artist who appears not to be an artist at all; the down-and-out clown who manages to stumble along life's tightrope, forever nearly yet never quite falling off: "Carlos, go on! Be *gauche* in life!" Drummond tells himself in the opening line of his first book of poems, self-effacingly entitled *Some Poetry.* For this "Carlos," the poet is determined to be the aerialist as Everyman; he wants to assure us how perfectly safe we are up there— that poetry is nothing to be afraid of; that if poetry is a problem it is to be *his* problem, not our own:

> World, wide world,
> if my name were Harold
> it might be a rhyme,
> but no answer.

"Seven-Sided Poem," tr. Mark Strand

The artlessness is deceptive, of course, for the poet carefully camouflages the sophistication of his art behind the naïveté of his poetic persona. It is a technique that Jorge Luis Borges first uncovered in Whitman (that great precursor of modern personae), and the Argentine writer's stricture applies equally here: The maladroit confessional poet of Drummond's verses would certainly be incapable of writing the poems that so cogently depict him.

In fact few confessional poets have told us less about themselves more convincingly. We know that he was born on October 31, 1902, in the small mining town of Itabira, in the interior of the landlocked state of Minas Gerais; that he was the son of a rancher ("The man behind the moustache/ . . . serious, simple, and strong. He hardly ever speaks."); that he went to boarding school in Belo Horizonte, the capital of Minas Gerais, and later to a Jesuit school in the state of Rio de Janeiro, from which he was eventually expelled for "mental insubordination," as he laconically describes it in one of his rare autobiographical disclosures.

The great risk of confessional poetry lies always in saying too much about oneself. Even the hyperbolic Whitman is careful to avoid this pitfall, by generally pretending to be ubiquitous and plural, by bear-hugging the reader and whisking him back and forth across the continent until he is too breathless to examine the truth of Walt's epic intimacies. Drummond proposes a far more subtle journey, filled with pathos and humor tinged with irony:

> Stepping on books and letters
> we travel in the family.
> Marriages; mortgages;
> the consumptive cousins;
> the mad aunt; my grandmother
> betrayed among the slave-girls,
> rustling silks in the bedroom.
> But he didn't say anything.

("Travelling in the Family," tr. E. Bishop)

The intention of his persona is less to confide in the reader than to inspire the reader's own confiding. For Drummond's confessions are more emblematic than autobiographical, providing the reader with an archetypal framework by which to investigate his or her own psyche. It is the disturbing phenomenon of life's poetry that is shared here, in the face of which the poet becomes just another spectator equally perplexed by the show:

> Carlos, keep calm, love
> is what you're seeing now:
> today a kiss, tomorrow no kiss,
> day after tomorrow's Sunday
> and nobody knows what will happen
> Monday.

("Don't Kill Yourself," tr. E. Bishop)

To understand the underpinnings of this timid, bumbling, slightly voyeuristic persona, to appreciate his suspicion of poetry and yearning for a common ground with the reader, it may be helpful to have some idea of the period in which this "Carlos" was engendered: the 1920's of Brazilian Modernism. Like most of the world in the early twentieth century, Brazil was bent upon shedding the previous hundred years once and for all. In poetry, Symbolism and Parnassianism had taken traditional verse about as far as it could go: to the cellar or the attic. Poetry was in mothballs. The whole of Latin America was exasperated with its centuries of fidelity to European tradition. Economically and politically, the axis of power in Brazil was shifting from a tired agricultural aristocracy to a new industrial class; this was thanks in part to World War I, which made the country a producer for the hungry warring economies of the older industrial world. Its population was also on the move, from the country to the city, and no urban center was growing faster than S ão Paulo, capital of coffee and commerce.

A Modern Art Week was held in São Paulo in February 1922, reflecting the vanguard movements in art, music and literature, especially poetry. Much as New York's Armory Show of 1913 had done for North American intellectuals, the event in Brazil not only introduced the European ferment of Cubism, Futurism, Dadaism and the like to an entire artistic generation but also provoked an identity crisis at home. A tremendous sense of emerging national identity was taking hold of Brazil at the time. In its most extreme cultural manifestations it would produce radical movements like *Antropofagia* or "Cannibalism" (Oswald de Andrade, "Tupi or not Tupi, that is the question!") that combined surrealism with primitivism in a kind of psycho-anthropological quest for Brazil's roots in pre-Columbian society—something Paz was to attempt later for Mexico. In poetry, Mário de Andrade would explore the history of Portuguese verse forms, popular and erudite, and their relationship to music, from the medieval lyric to Amazonian tribal rituals. Drummond captured an entire society in a state of flux: "prayers,/victrolas,/saints crossing themselves,/ads for a better soap,/a racket of which nobody/knows the why or wherefore." Traditional poetry became a joke: "But this moon/and this brandy/play the devil with one's emotions." Nothing was sacred: "Oh, let us be pornographic! (Sweetly, sweetly pornographic!)."

In 1925, an already reticent Drummond helped to start a Modernist journal in Minas Gerais. Unlike magazines such as Mário's *Klaxon* and Oswald's *Revista de Antropofagia,* which were proclaiming "revolution" in São Paulo, it was modestly entitled *The Review.* That same year, Drummond married and obtained a degree in pharmacology. By 1929, he had become a civil servant in the Department of Education, as well as a journalist. The following year he published his first book of poems. In 1934, Drummond moved to Rio, where for the next fifty years he would quietly exercise his quadruple vocation of poet, journalist, bureaucrat and translator (of Balzac, Hamsun, Laclos, Lorca, Maeterlinck, Mau-

riac, Molière and Proust), interrupted only by his retirement from the
civil service in 1962.

Drummond would later look back on this period of literary upheaval
(in one of the few autobiographical pieces he has allowed himself to
write) with a certain irony:

My first book, *Some Poetry* (1923–1930), shows a great inexperience in
suffering and an ingenuous delight in the individual as such. Already, with
*Wasteland of Souls* (1931–1934), there is something ordered, structured.
The individualism has become exacerbated, but there is also a growing
consciousness of its own precariousness and a tacit critique of the spiritual
conduct (or absence thereof) of the author. I think the elementary contra-
dictions in my poetry resolved themselves in a third volume, *Feeling for
the World* (1935–1940). Only the elementary ones, mind you . . .

This passage was written in 1944, and what had intruded was not only
his father's death in 1931 but seemingly an entire world. The familial
and artistic innocence of the early persona was to suffer profound mod-
ification:

> Father dead, loved one dead.
> Aunt dead, brother born dead.
> Cousins dead, friend dead.
> Grandfather dead, mother dead
> (hands white, portrait on the wall always
>     crooked, speck of dust in the eyes).
> Acquaintances dead, teacher dead.
>
> Enemy dead.
>
> Fiancée dead, girl friends dead.
> Engineer dead, passenger dead.
> Unrecognizable body dead: a man's? an animal's?
> Dog dead, bird dead.
> Rosebush dead, orange trees dead.
> Air dead, bay dead.
> Hope, patience, eyes, sleep, movement of hands:
>     dead.
>
>              ("Motionless Faces," tr. Mark Strand)

In an essay on "Three Romantic Poets" from this same period, remark-
ing on the "touching vulgarity" of Casimiro de Abreu's poetry, Drum-

mond summarized the banality that makes everything about Abreu's work so familiar to the reader:

a) man remembers his childhood and grows sad.
b) man experiences an unattainable love and grows sad.
c) man is far from home and feels nostalgic.

The list might serve as a synopsis of Drummond's maturing persona, if one were to add an additional theme:

d) man looks at the world around him and grows even sadder.

It is from this "Feeling about the World," as he calls it, that the "tabloid" biographies of "Luisa Porto" or "Phantom Girl" now emerge:

> I am the girl you loved
> who died of sickness,
> who died in a car crash,
> who killed herself on the beach,
> whose hair stayed
> long in your memory.
>
> ("Song of the Phantom Girl of Belo
> Horizonte," tr. Mark Strand)

At the same time, his disappointment with the world begins to turn an already reticent persona more and more inward:

> For many years I lived in Itabira.
> Basically I come from Itabira.
> That's why I'm sad, proud—ironclad.
> Ninety percent iron in the sidewalks.
> Eighty percent iron in the soul.
> And this detachment from whatever in life is porous
>     and communicative.
>
> ("Itabiran Confession," tr. Thomas Colchie)

A deeper struggle gradually unfolds, one aimed at salvaging poetry itself, that once-splendid edifice that has fallen into ruin, that broken-down "grand hotel of the world" which can barely be glimpsed beneath the scaffolding:

The slow and crimson alexandrine decomposed.
Couples coupling together in the whispering
Carioca smut, streetcars sparksmelling, politicians
politicianing along insipid corridors
Italian starlets, doormen in ecstasy
    elevator
boys in a panic:
how is such voluptuousness to fit itself
into those four flimsy paneled partitions?

("To a Hotel Scheduled for Demolition," tr. Thomas Colchie)

For over half a century Carlos Drummond de Andrade has attempted to reconstruct poetry and its relationship to the recurring themes of The Individual, Home, Family, Friends, Social Impact, Amorous Experience, Poetry Itself, Playful Exercises and Vision of (or Experiment in) Existence, these being the headings he uses to organize his "Personal Anthology," published in 1962. It is this meticulous recasting of poetry's basic themes that has made Drummond the most influential modern poet Brazil or, for that matter, the Portuguese world has produced in this century—and not simply, as his "Carlos" concluded enigmatically in his own *Autobiography:*

. . . the confessed author of a certain poem, insignificant in itself, but which from 1928 on has continued to scandalize my age; and which even today to divide people in Brazil into two mental categories:

In the middle of the road was a stone
was a stone in the middle of the road
was a stone
in the middle of the road was a stone.
I'll never get over that happening
in the life of my wearied retinas.
I'll never get over how in the middle of the road
was a stone
was a stone in the middle of the road
in the middle of the road was a stone.

("In the Middle of the Road," tr. Thomas Colchie)

—THOMAS COLCHIE<br>
February 1986

# *from* ALGUMA POESIA

## (Some Poetry)

### 1930

# SEVEN-SIDED POEM

When I was born, one of the crooked
angels who live in shadow, said:
Carlos, go on! Be *gauche* in life.

The houses watch the men,
men who run after women.
If the afternoon had been blue,
there might have been less desire.

The trolley goes by full of legs:
white legs, black legs, yellow legs.
My God, why all the legs?
my heart asks. But my eyes
ask nothing at all.

The man behind the moustache
is serious, simple, and strong.
He hardly ever speaks.
He has a few, choice friends,
the man behind the spectacles and the moustache.

My God, why hast Thou forsaken me
if Thou knew'st I was not God,
if Thou knew'st that I was weak?

Universe, vast universe,
if I had been named Eugene
that would not be what I mean
but it would go into verse
faster.

Universe, vast universe,
my heart is vaster.*

I oughtn't to tell you,
but this moon
and this brandy
play the devil with one's emotions.
E. B.

# INFANCY

My father got on his horse and went to the field.
My mother stayed sitting and sewing.
My little brother slept.
A small boy alone under the mango trees,
I read the story of Robinson Crusoe,
the long story that never comes to an end.

At noon, white with light, a voice that had learned
lullabies long ago in the slave-quarters—and never forgot—
called us for coffee.
Coffee blacker than the black old woman
delicious coffee
good coffee.

My mother stayed sitting and sewing
watching me:
*Shh*—don't wake the boy.
She stopped the cradle when a mosquito had lit
and gave a sigh . . . how deep!
Away off there my father went riding
through the farm's endless wastes.

And I didn't know that my story
was prettier than that of Robinson Crusoe.

E. B.

# THE MARRIAGE OF HEAVEN AND HELL

Against the sky of methylene blue
an ironic
diuretic moon
hangs like a picture for a dining room.

Guardian angels on their nightly rounds
rock pubescent slumbers,
shooing away mosquitoes
from draperies and swags.

All along the spiral stairs
are the runaway virgins
—blinking like fireflies—
incorporated into the Milky Way.

Through a crack
peeks the Devil, squinting one eye.

The Devil has his spyglass
to peer from seven leagues' off,
and an ear as subtle
as the finest violin.

Saint Peter snores
to the measured tock of the heavenly clock.

The Devil peeks through a crack.

Far down below
bruised lips sigh.
Sighing prayers? Sighing softly,
for love.

And limbs, intertwined,
become more entwined
as flesh penetrates flesh.

God's will be done!
But for Laura, and Beatrice
perhaps, the rest are lost . . .
T. C.

# IN THE MIDDLE OF THE ROAD

In the middle of the road there was a stone
there was a stone in the middle of the road
there was a stone
in the middle of the road there was a stone.

Never should I forget this event
in the life of my fatigued retinas.
Never should I forget that in the middle of the road
there was a stone
there was a stone in the middle of the road
in the middle of the road there was a stone.

E. B.

# QUADRILLE

John loved Teresa who loved Raymond
who loved Mary who loved Jack who loved Lily
who didn't love anybody.
John went to the United States, Teresa
    to a convent
Raymond died in an accident, Mary became
    an old maid,
Jack committed suicide and Lily married J.
    Pinto Fernandez
who didn't figure into the story.
M. S.

# THE ONSET OF LOVE

The hammock between two mango trees
swayed in the sunken world.
It was hot, windless.
Above was the sun,
between were leaves.
It was broiling.

And since I had nothing to do, I developed a passion
      for the legs of the laundress.

One day she came to the hammock,
curled up in my arms,
gave me a hug,
gave me her breasts
that were just for me.
The hammock turned over,
down went the world.

And I went to bed
with a fever of forty degrees.
And a giant laundress with giant breasts was spinning
      around in the greenness of space.

M. S.

# BALLAD OF LOVE THROUGH THE AGES

From the beginning of time,
I liked you, you liked me.
I was Greek, you were Trojan,
Trojan but not Helen.
I sprung from a wooden horse
to kill your brother.
I killed, we quarreled, we died.

I became a Roman soldier,
persecutor of Christians.
At the catacomb door
I met you again.
But when I saw you fall
naked in the Colosseum
and the lion coming toward you,
I made a desperate leap
and the lion ate us both.

Next I was a Moorish pirate,
the scourge of Tripoli.
I set fire to the frigate
where you were hiding from
the fury of my brigantine.
But when I went to grab you
and take you as my slave,
you crossed yourself and drove
a dagger through your heart.
I killed myself as well.

Later on, in happier days,
I was a courtier at Versailles,
clever and debauched.
You dreamed of being a nun . . .

I vaulted over the convent wall
but difficult politics
led us to the guillotine.

These days I'm totally modern:
dancing, jogging, working out.
And I have money in the bank.
And you're a fabulous blonde:
dancing, jogging, working out.
None of it pleases your father.
But after a thousand reversals,
I, one of Paramount's heroes,
give you a hug, a kiss, and we marry.

M. S.

# SIESTA

The family from Minas
relaxes in the sun
happy and silent
out on the grass.
The youngest boy
is staring into the sky
not at the sun
but a bower of bananas.
Cut some down, Father.
The father lops off a bunch
and offers them to everyone.
The family from Minas
sits eating bananas.

The eldest girl
scratches an insect bite
high above her knee.
The skirt exposes
her well-built
dusky thigh
but no one notices.
Their eyes are lost
to the undulating line
of the nearby horizon
(a garden fence).
The family from Minas
is gazing inward.

The eldest boy
is humming a melody
not happy or sad
but softly enough
to lull them to sleep.

Only a buzzing mosquito
displays any restlessness.
The youngest boy
lifts his sluggish hand
to swat away the intruder.
The family from Minas
lies sleeping in the sun.

T. C.

14

*from* BREJO DAS
ALMAS

*(Wasteland of Souls)*

*1934*

# DAWN

The poet rode the trolley drunk.
The sun came up behind the yards.
The small hotels slept very sadly.
The houses too were drunk.

Everything was a total wreck.
Nobody knew that the world was going to end
(only a child did but kept it quiet),
that the world was going to end at 7:45.
Last thoughts! Last telegrams!

Joe who listed pronouns,
Helen who loved men,
Sebastian who ruined himself,
Arthur who never said anything,
set off for eternity.

The poet is drunk, but
he hears a voice in the dawn:
Why don't we all go dancing
between the trolley and the tree?

Between the trolley and the tree
dance, brothers!
Even without music
dance, brothers!
Children are being born
with so much spontaneity.
Love is fantastic
(love and what it produces).
Dance, brothers!
Death will come later
like a sacrament.

M. S.

# IN THE LIGHT OF RECENT EVENTS

Oh, let us be pornographic!
(Sweetly, sweetly pornographic!)
Why be more immaculate
than our Portuguese progenitors?

Oh, let us be warriors,
navigators and explorers;
let us be all we want
but, above all, pornographic.

The evening may ache
and the women look sad
like a punch in the eye
(pornographic, pornographic).

Your friends may smile
at your latest resolution
—they thought that suicide
was your ultimate solution.
They fail to grasp, poor fools,
why it's best to be pornographic.

Recommend it to your neighbors,
to the conductor on your train,
and to all the other creatures,
superfluous but alive;
propose it to the man wearing the glasses,
to the woman toting her bundle of clothes.
Go tell them all: Dear brothers,
don't you want to be pornographic?

T. C.

# DON'T KILL YOURSELF

Carlos, keep calm, love
is what you're seeing now:
today a kiss, tomorrow no kiss,
day after tomorrow's Sunday
and nobody knows what will happen
Monday.

It's useless to resist
or to commit suicide.
Don't kill yourself. Don't kill yourself!
Keep all of yourself for the nuptials
coming nobody knows when,
that is, if they ever come.

Love, Carlos, tellurian,
spent the night with you,
and now your insides are raising
an ineffable racket,
prayers,
victrolas,
saints crossing themselves,
ads for a better soap,
a racket of which nobody
knows the why or wherefore.

In the meantime you go on your way
vertical, melancholy.
You're the palm tree, you're the cry
nobody heard in the theatre
and all the lights went out.
Love in the dark, no, love
in the daylight, is always sad,

sad, Carlos, my boy,
but tell it to nobody,
nobody knows nor shall know.

E. B.

*from*

# SENTIMENTO DO MUNDO

## *(A Feeling About the World)*

### *1940*

# ITABIRAN CONFESSION

For many years I lived in Itabira.
Basically I come from Itabira.
That's why I'm sad, proud—ironclad.
Ninety percent iron in the sidewalks.
Eighty percent iron in the soul.
And this detachment from whatever in life is porous and
    communicative.

The aching for love that frustrates my work
also comes from Itabira: from its white nights without women
    or horizon.
And that habit of suffering which so humors me
is a pure Itabiran legacy.

Have a look at my mementos, collected in Itabira.
This Saint Benedict, carved by old Alfredo Duval.
And my tapir hide, draped over the parlor sofa.
Not to mention this pride, this lowered head . . .

I used to have gold, cattle, ranches.
Today I'm a civil servant.
Itabira's nothing more than the photograph on the wall.
But how it lingers!

T. C.

# SONG OF THE PHANTOM GIRL OF
# BELO HORIZONTE

I am the phantom girl
who waits on Chumbo Street
for the coach of dawn.
I am white and tall and cold,
my flesh is a sigh
in the mountain dawn.
I am the phantom girl.
My name was Maria,
Maria-Who-Died.

I am the girl you loved
who died of sickness,
who died in a car crash,
who killed herself on the beach,
whose hair stayed
long in your memory.
I was never of this world:
when kissed, my mouth
spoke of other planets
where lovers burn
in a chaste fire
and without irony
turn into stars.

Unlike the others, I died
without having time to be yours.
I cannot get used to this,
and when the police are asleep
in and around me,
my wandering ghost
goes down Curral Hill,
spying on the new houses,
circling the lovers' gardens

(Cláudio Manuel da Costa Street),
stopping for shelter in the Hotel Ceará
that offers no shelter. A perfume
I do not know invades me:
it is the odor of your sleep,
soft and warm, curled up
in the arms of Spanish women . . .
Oh! Let me sleep with you!

My ghost keeps going,
for I meet none of my lovers,
who were seduced by French women,
who drank all the whisky
in Brasil
(and are now in a drunken sleep),
and meet only cars that pass
with drivers who, surprised
by my whiteness, flee.
The shy policemen,
poor things! One wanted to grab me.
I opened my arms. . . . Incredulous,
he felt me. There was no flesh
and outside the dress
and under the dress
the same white absence,
a white anguish . . .
It is obvious: what was body
was eaten by the cat.

The girls that are still alive
(they'll die, you can be sure)
are afraid that I'll appear
and pull them down by their legs . . .
        They're wrong.
I was a girl, I will be a girl
deserted, *per omnia saecula.*
I have no interest in girls.
Boys disturb me.
I don't know how to free myself.
If only my ghost wouldn't suffer,

if only they would still like me.
If only the spirit would consent,
but I know it's forbidden,
you are flesh, I am mist.

A mist that dissolves
when the sun breaks in the mountains.

Now I feel better,
I've said everything I wanted to,
I would climb that cloud,
be a frozen sheet
sparkling over mankind.
But the stars will not understand,
nobody will understand,
my reflection in the pool
on Paráuna Avenue.

M. S.

# BOY CRYING IN THE NIGHT

In the warm, humid night, noiseless and dead, a boy cries.
His crying behind the wall, the light behind the window
are lost in the shadow of muffled footsteps, of tired voices.
Yet the sound of medicine poured into a spoon can be heard.

A boy cries in the night, behind the wall, across the street,
far away a boy cries, in another city,
in another world, perhaps.

And I see the hand that lifts the spoon while the other holds the
    head,
and I see the slick thread run down the boy's chin,
and slip into the street, only a thread, and slip through the city.
And nobody else in the world exists but that boy crying.
M. S.

# THE DEAD IN FROCK COATS

In the corner of the living room was an album
    of unbearable photos,
many meters high and infinite minutes old,
over which everyone leaned
making fun of the dead in frock coats.

Then a worm began to chew the indifferent coats,
the pages, the inscriptions, and even the dust
    on the pictures.
The only thing it did not chew was the ever-
    lasting sob of life that broke
and broke from those pages.

M. S.

# YOUR SHOULDERS HOLD UP
# THE WORLD

A time comes when you no longer can say:
    my God.
A time of total cleaning up.
A time when you no longer can say: my love.
Because love proved useless.
And the eyes don't cry.
And the hands do only rough work.
And the heart is dry.

Women knock at your door in vain, you won't open.
You remain alone, the light turned off,
and your enormous eyes shine in the dark.
It is obvious you no longer know how to suffer.
And you want nothing from your friends.

Who cares if old age comes, what is old age?
Your shoulders are holding up the world
and it's lighter than a child's hand.
Wars, famine, family fights inside buildings
prove only that life goes on
and not everybody has freed himself yet.
Some (the delicate ones) judging the spectacle cruel
will prefer to die.
A time comes when death doesn't help.
A time comes when life is an order.
Just life, without any escapes.
M. S.

29

# SOUVENIR OF THE ANCIENT WORLD

Clara strolled in the garden with the children.
The sky was green over the grass,
the water was golden under the bridges,
other elements were blue and rose and orange,
a policeman smiled, bicycles passed,
a girl stepped onto the lawn to catch a bird,
the whole world—Germany, China—
        all was quiet around Clara.

The children looked at the sky: it was not forbidden.
Mouth, nose, eyes were open. There was no
        danger.
What Clara feared were the flu, the heat, the
        insects.
Clara feared missing the eleven o'clock trolley:
She waited for letters slow to arrive,
She couldn't always wear a new dress. But
        she strolled in the garden, in the morning!
They had gardens, they had mornings in those days!

M. S.

# *from* JOSÉ

## 1942

# THE EDIFICE

## I

In the sand on a beach
Oscar traces its design:
soon The Splendor rises
above a beach of sand.

With cement, the myth of
human frailty vanishes
as families are dispatched
to imperturbable cells.

Through monotonous doors
the elevator blandly
discharges, absorbs
their corporeal ranks.

It's years ago since
we did away with man.
Now, rueful inhabitants
are all that remain.

## I I

Oh, secret life of lock and key:
bodies joining, unjoining
—abruptly, they separate.

The blues with a glass of whiskey
quickly distills emergency opiates.
Only the portrait on the wall
a thorn in the heart
some fruit on the piano

and a breeze off the coast that smells of seaweed,
    sadness, distance . . .

How good to fall in or out of love,
to bite, to moan, to agonize.
How good to suffer and lie!
What can rain matter to the ocean?
To the earth? To the flames?
The tread of feet—what difference?
The furniture still laughed, as night fell.
The world still wilted, bloomed
to each spiraling of an embrace.

And sure enough it came, surreptitiously,
in moments of carnal weariness
that pang of remorse for a lost Goiás
. . . land of extinct purity.

As the portrait on the wall stroked his mustache.

### I I I

How it aches within me
that house of long ago.
It was idle, calm, white
with winding corridors
and in its thirty doorways
stood thirty smiling maids.
Naked? I can't remember.

It was filled with ghosts
souls without benediction
guardian angels, Indian slings
and great tins of sweets
and great sighs of love
as we later discovered.

Weep, portrait, weep!
While your whiskers grow
in this grim edifice

where childhood looms
like a poisoned cup.

## IV

The complicated gas installations
perfect for suicide.
A terrace for hanging shirts
is a possible alternative.
That fear of coffins
lurking in the elevator.
The extravagant bathroom
in a thousand Moorish shades
where the body pales
with slack disgust
at its earlier lasciviousness.

Ah, the body, my body
what will become of it?
My one and only trunk
the one made of milk
the one made of air
of water, of flesh.
The one dressed in black,
in white, in beige;
the one I coiffed in hats
and shod with boots;
cared for, cajoled,
enveloped with defenses.

My homely, homely body
so forsaken up here
in the wind, in the clouds
of this airy living room.

## V

The carpets soon faded
worn out by other feet.

Music would drift up amid
the rumor of casino chips.

A breeze hovered softly
in the curtains before dawn.

The lives, long discarded,
now returned by the window.

Father, Alberto, grandfather,
the dead present themselves.

No need to switch on a light
with those trembling hands.

To drink or smoke is forbidden
so they eye each other in silence.

The portrait has dimmed
to a dusty gray veneer.

Debts slowly mounted.
Rain fell for twenty years.

Ludicrous customs evolved
and even stranger vices.

"What a century, my God!" concluded the rats
as they began to eat the edifice.

T. C.

# MOTIONLESS FACES

Father dead, loved one dead.
Aunt dead, brother born dead.
Cousins dead, friend dead.
Grandfather dead, mother dead
(hands white, portrait on the wall always
    crooked, speck of dust in the eyes).
Acquaintances dead, teacher dead.

Enemy dead.

Fiancée dead, girl friends dead.
Engineer dead, passenger dead.
Unrecognizable body dead: a man's? an animal's?
Dog dead, bird dead.
Rosebush dead, orange trees dead.
Air dead, bay dead.
Hope, patience, eyes, sleep, movement of hands:
    dead.

Man dead. Lights go on.
He works at night as if he were living.

Good morning! He is stronger (as if he were living).

Dead without an obituary, secretly dead.
He knows how to imitate hunger, and how to
    pretend to love.

And how to insist on walking, and how well
    he walks.
He could walk through walls, but he uses doors.

His pale hand says good-bye to Russia.
Time enters and leaves him endlessly.

The dead pass quickly; they cannot be held on to.
As soon as one leaves, another one is tapping
      your shoulder.
I woke up and saw the city:
the dead were like machines,
the houses belonged to the dead,
drowsy waves,
an exhausted chest smelling of lilies,
feet bound up.
I slept and went to the city:
everything was burning,
crackling of bamboo,
mouth dry, suddenly puckering.
I dreamt and returned to the city.
But it wasn't the city anymore.
They were all dead, the medical examiner was
      checking the tags on the corpses.
The medical examiner himself had died years ago
      but his hand continued implacably.
The awful stench was everywhere.

From this veranda without a railing I watch both
      twilights.
I watch my life running away with a wolf's
      speed, I want to stop it, but would I
      be bitten?
I look at my feet, how they have grown, flies
      circulate among them.
I look at everything and add it up, nothing is
      left, I am poor, poor, poor,
but I cannot enter the circle,
I cannot remain alone,
I shall kiss everyone on the forehead,
I shall distribute moist flowers,
after . . . There is no after or before.
There is cold on all sides,
and a central cold, whiter still.

Colder still . . .
A whiteness that pays well our old anger
        and bitterness . . .
Feeling myself so clear among you, kissing you
        and getting no dust in my mouth or face.
Peace of wispy trees,
of fragile mountains down below, of timid river-
        banks, of gestures that can no longer annoy,
sweet peace without eyes, in the dark, in the air.
Sweet peace within me,
within my family that came from a fog unbroken
        by the sun
and returns to their islands by underground roads,
in my street, in my time—finally—reconciled,
in the city of my birth, in my rented rooms,
in my life, in everyone's life, in the mild and
        deep death of myself and everyone.
M. S.

# JOSÉ

What now, José?
The party's over,
the lights are out,
the people are gone,
the night is cold,
what now, José?
what do you say?
nameless José,
who teases others,
who makes up verses,
who loves? Who quarrels?
what now, José?

You have no woman,
you've run out of words,
you've run out of love,
you can't drink anymore,
you can't smoke anymore,
you can't even spit,
the night is cold,
the day's not come,
the trolley's not come,
not come is utopia
and nobody's laughing
and everything's over
and everything's gone
and everything's stale,
what now José?

What now, José?
Your sweet talk,
your feasting and fasting,
your moment of fever,

your books,
your gold mines,
your suit of glass,
your incoherence,
your anger—what now?

The key's in your hand,
you want to open the door,
there is no door;
you want to die in the sea,
the sea dried up;
you want to go to Minas,
Minas is gone;
José, what now?

If you screamed,
if you wailed,
if you played
a Vienna waltz,
if you slept,
if you tired,
if you died . . .
But you won't,
you're tough, José!

Alone in the dark
like a wild animal,
without a theogony,
without a bare wall
to lean on,
without a black horse
to ride off on,
you march, José!
But where, José?

M. S.

41

# THE DIRTY HAND

My hand is dirty.
I must cut it off.
To wash it is pointless.
The water is putrid.
The soap is bad.
It won't lather.
The hand is dirty.
It's been dirty for years.

I used to keep it
out of sight,
in my pants pocket.
No one suspected a thing.
People came up to me,
wanting to shake hands.
I would refuse.
and the hidden hand
would leave its imprint
on my thigh.
And I saw
it was the same
if I used it or not.
Disgust was the same.

How many nights
in the depths of the house
I washed that hand,
scrubbed it, polished it,
dreamed it would turn
to diamond or crystal
or even, at last,
into a plain white hand,
the clean hand of a man,

that you could shake,
or kiss, or hold
in one of those moments
when two people confess
without saying a word . . .
Only to have
the incurable hand
open its dirty fingers.

And the dirt was vile.
It was not mud or soot
or the caked filth
of an old scab
or the sweat
of a laborer's shirt.
It was a sad dirt
made of sickness
and human anguish.
It was not black;
black is pure.
It was dull,
a dull grayish dirt.
It is impossible
to live with this
gross hand that lies
on the table.
Quick! Cut it off!
Chop it to pieces
and throw it
into the ocean.
With time, with hope
and its intricate workings
another hand will come,
pure, transparent as glass,
and fasten itself to my arm.
M. S.

# TRAVELLING IN THE FAMILY

*To Rodrigo M. F. de Andrade*

In the desert of Itabira
the shadow of my father
took me by the hand.
So much time lost.
But he didn't say anything.
It was neither day nor night.
A sigh? A passing bird?
But he didn't say anything.

We have come a long way.
Here there was a house.
The mountain used to be bigger.
So many heaped-up dead,
and time gnawing the dead.
And in the ruined houses,
cold disdain and damp.
But he didn't say anything.

The street he used to cross
on horseback, at a gallop.
His watch. His clothes.
His legal documents.
His tales of love-affairs.
Opening of tin trunks
and violent memories.
But he didn't say anything.

In the desert of Itabira
things come back to life,
stiflingly, suddenly.
The market of desires
displays its sad treasures;
my urge to run away;

naked women; remorse.
But he didn't say anything.

Stepping on books and letters
we travel in the family.
Marriages; mortgages;
the consumptive cousins;
the mad aunt; my grandmother
betrayed among the slave-girls,
rustling silks in the bedroom.
But he didn't say anything.

What cruel, obscure instinct
moved his pallid hand
subtly pushing us
into the forbidden
time, forbidden places?

I looked in his white eyes.
I cried to him: Speak! My voice
shook in the air a moment,
beat on the stones. The shadow
proceeded slowly on
with that pathetic travelling
across the lost kingdom.
But he didn't say anything.

I saw grief, misunderstanding
and more than one old revolt
dividing us in the dark.
The hand I wouldn't kiss,
the crumb that they denied me,
refusal to ask pardon.
Pride. Terror at night.
But he didn't say anything.

Speak speak speak speak.
I pulled him by his coat
that was turning into clay.
By the hands, by the boots

I caught at his strict shadow
and the shadow released itself
with neither haste nor anger.
But he remained silent.

There were distinct silences
deep within his silence.
There was my deaf grandfather
hearing the painted birds
on the ceiling of the church;
my own lack of friends;
and your lack of kisses;
there were our difficult lives
and a great separation
in the little space of the room.

The narrow space of life
crowds me up against you,
and in this ghostly embrace
it's as if I were being burned
completely, with poignant love.
Only now do we know each other!
Eye-glasses, memories, portraits
flow in the river of blood.
Now the waters won't let me
make out your distant face,
distant by seventy years . . .

I felt that he pardoned me
but he didn't say anything.
The waters cover his moustache,
the family, Itabira, all.

E. B.

*from* A ROSA
DO POVO

*(Rose of the People)*

*1945*

# LOOKING FOR POETRY

Don't write poems about what's happening.
Nothing is born or dies in poetry's presence.
Next to it, life is a static sun
without warmth or light.
Friendships, birthdays, personal matters don't count.
Don't write poems with the body,
that excellent, whole, and comfortable body objects to lyrical
    outpouring.
Your anger, your grimace of pleasure or pain in the dark
mean nothing.
Don't show off your feelings
that are slow in coming around and take advantage of doubt.
What you think and feel are not poetry yet.

Don't sing about your city, leave it in peace.
Song is not the movement of machines or the secret of houses.
It is not music heard in passing, noise of the sea in streets that
    skirt the borders of foam.
Song is not nature
or men in society.
Rain and night, fatigue and hope, mean nothing to it.
Poetry (you don't get it from things)
leaves out subject and object.

Don't dramatize, don't invoke,
don't question, don't waste time lying.
Don't get upset.
Your ivory yacht, your diamond shoe,
your mazurkas and tirades, your family skeletons,
all of them worthless, disappear in the curve of time.

Don't bring up
your sad and buried childhood.

Don't waver between the mirror
and a fading memory.
What faded was not poetry.
What broke was not crystal.

Enter the kingdom of words as if you were deaf.
Poems are there that want to be written.
They are dormant, but don't be let down,
their virginal surfaces are fresh and serene.
They are alone and mute, in dictionary condition.
Live with your poems before you write them.
If they're vague, be patient. If they offend, be calm.
Wait until each one comes into its own and demolishes
with its command of words
and its command of silence.
Don't force poems to let go of limbo.
Don't pick up lost poems from the ground.
Don't fawn over poems. Accept them
as you would their final and definitive form,
distilled in space.

Come close and consider the words.
With a plain face hiding thousands of other faces
and with no interest in your response,
whether weak or strong,
each word asks:
Did you bring the key?

Take note:
words hide in the night
in caves of music and image.
Still humid and pregnant with sleep
they turn in a winding river and by neglect are transformed.
M. S.

# THE PACKAGE

It's the small package
I've carried with me
these dozens of years
these hundreds of years.

A couple of letters?
It might be a flower
a portrait, perhaps,
or even a handkerchief.

I don't know where
I found it,
if it was stolen
or came as a gift.

Did angels descend
with it in hand?
Was it bobbing in the river?
Did it soar through the air?

Whatever it contains
or whether it contains
anything, I can't tell.
I don't dare unwrap it.

The idea alone is more
than I can contemplate
the package is so cold
and yet—so hot.

It burns in the hand
it's soft to the touch

it often thrills me
then leaves me sad.

To keep a secret
to and from oneself:
not wanting to know
or wanting too much.

To keep a secret
out of sight
behind memory
beyond sleep.

(The practiced mouth
hails friends, "Hello!"
the heart swells up
hand shaking hand.)

Calls rise from the sea
from all things, alarm!
The world summons you
Carlos! No answer?

I want to answer!
The infinite road
winds past the sea.
I want to take it.

The package is heavy
the temptation strong
to toss it down
the nearest hole.

Or why not burn it?
With the ashes scattered
all trace will vanish
along with remorse.

Ah, subtle weight
that, rather than be

carried, carries me
—yes, but where?

Won't you share,
intolerable burden,
the cruel word
hidden in your heart?

To follow you meekly
on so long a journey
with no explanation
except that I follow.

If you'd just open up
to reveal yourself
even as a mistake—
what a consolation!

But you stay closed . . .
though I take you along
to the evening dance
and each morning we ride

to the dim factory
of a mournful suburb.
In a way, we're friends
openly, and in secret.

To lose you, for me,
would be to lose myself
I'm someone free
but I carry something.

Something indescribable:
I didn't choose it
I haven't seen it
yet I carry something.

Whatever it may be
I'm never empty
I'm not alone.
Something's with me.
T. C.

# IN THE GOLDEN AGE

In the golden age
the road was all.
On the right side
were gardens
we would enter
only to exit
on the left,
the left was always
guarded by fences.
This would happen
a thousand times.

For the room
to be elsewhere
only a candle was needed.
Our faces were
buried in books
forever it seemed.
And the key to the cellar
was ours, like the un-
forgettable girl
of the waterfall,
bathing within us,
space and vision
were multiplied
in the golden age.

In the golden age
that was really copper
there were many nights
of pouring rain.
An awful palm
fed up with the city

went to the jungle.
And after the mail
came the assassin.
Africa's wealth
was lost in the wind.
And it was hard
to be a young boy.

Just on the verge
of modern times,
we were held up
while gardens
of sickness,
streetcars of boredom,
stores of tears,
all prospered.
Space is small.
Things pile up.
And making the rounds,
from hand to hand
goes a sealed
white paper,
the plan, perhaps,
of the golden age.

In the golden age
that sleeps on the floor
about to wake up,
I tried to discover
distant roads,
early rivers,
genuine trust,
and superlative poems.
Whenever it's asked
that these things be explained
I haven't the strength.
The trick is to wait.

In the golden age
my heart smiling,

my eyes like diamonds,
my lips keeping time
to some pure song.
In the town market
I sense the new clothes
and I hear the flags
spill out on the air.

In the golden age
childhood comes back
in return for nothing
and space reopened
allows to vanish
the smallest men,
the brittlest things,
the needle, the trip,
the mouth's color,
allows to vanish
the oil of things,
allows to vanish
Saturdays' lawns,
allows to vanish
the paralytic dog,
allows to vanish
my sweetheart,
allows to vanish
the circle of water
reflecting the face . . .
Allows to vanish
the dull cloth,
holding her so
in the golden age.
M. S.

# RESIDUE

From everything a little remained.
From my fear. From your disgust.
From stifled cries. From the rose
a little remained.

A little remained of light
caught inside the hat.
In the eyes of the pimp
a little remained of tenderness,
very little.

A little remained of the dust
that covered your white shoes.
Of your clothes a little remained,
a few velvet rags, very
very few.

From everything a little remained.
From the bombed-out bridge,
from the two blades of grass,
from the empty pack
of cigarettes a little remained.

So from everything a little remains.
A little remains of your chin
in the chin of your daughter.

A little remained of your
blunt silence, a little
in the angry wall,
in the mute rising leaves.

A little remained from everything
in porcelain saucers,
in the broken dragon, in the white flowers,
in the creases of your brow,
in the portrait.

Since from everything a little remains,
why won't a little
of me remain? In the train
traveling north, in the ship,
in newspaper ads,
why not a little of me in London,
a little of me somewhere?
In a consonant?
In a well?

A little remains dangling
in the mouths of rivers,
just a little, and the fish
don't avoid it, which is very unusual.

From everything a little remains.
Not much: this absurd drop
dripping from the faucet,
half salt and half alcohol,
this frog leg jumping,
this watch crystal
broken into a thousand wishes,
this swan's neck,
this childhood secret . . .
From everything a little remained:
from me; from you; from Abelard.
Hair on my sleeve,
from everything a little remained;
wind in my ears,
burbing, rumbling
from an upset stomach,
and small artifacts:
bell jar, honeycomb, revolver
cartridge, aspirin tablet.

From everything a little remained.

And from everything a little remains.
Oh, open the bottles of lotion
and smother
the cruel, unbearable odor of memory.

Still, horribly, from everything a little remains,
under the rhythmic waves
under the clouds and the wind
under the bridges and under the tunnels
under the flames and under the sarcasm
under the phlegm and under the vomit
under the cry from the dungeon, the guy they
    forgot
under the spectacles and under the scarlet death
under the libraries, asylums, victorious churches
under yourself and under your feet already hard
under the ties of family, the ties of class,
from everything a little always remains.
Sometimes a button. Sometimes a rat.

M. S.

# STORY OF THE DRESS

Mother, whose dress is hanging
there on that nail?

Children, that is the dress
of a woman who is gone.

When did she go, Mother?
When did we know her?

Hold your tongues, children,
your father is coming.

Mother, say quickly
whose dress is that dress.

Children, her body is cold
and does not wear clothes.

The dress on that nail
is lifeless, is calm.

Listen, children,
to the words that I say.

There once was a woman
your father was mad for.

He was so much in love
that we could not reach him,

he cut himself off,
shut himself up,

devoured himself,
cried on the meat platter,

drank and quarreled,
and beat me up,

he left me behind with your cradle,
went to that woman,

but she didn't care.
Your father begged, but so what?

He gave her insurance, a farm,
gave her a car, gave her gold,

he would lap up her leavings,
would lick her shoes.

But she didn't care.
Your furious father

then asked me to ask
that devilish woman

if she would be patient
and sleep with him. . . .

Mother, why are you crying?
Take one of our handkerchiefs.

Children, be still,
your father's in the courtyard.

Mother, none of us heard
his foot on the stairs.

Children, I searched all over
for that demon-woman.

I begged her to yield

to my husband's will.

I don't love your husband,
she said with a laugh.

But I can stay with him,
if that's what you want,

just to please you, not me,
I don't want a man.

I looked at your father,
his eyes were pleading.

I looked at the woman,
her eyes were happy.

Her fancy dress
with its plunging neckline

showed more than it hid
of her sinner's parts.

I crossed myself,
I bowed . . . I said yes.

I left thinking of death,
but death did not come.

I walked the five streets,
by the bridge, by the river,

I went to your relatives,
did not eat, did not talk,

I had a high fever,
but death did not come.

The danger passed,
my hair had turned white,

I had lost my teeth,
my eyesight was gone,

I took in laundry,
I sewed, I made candy,

my hands were scarred,
my rings were broken,

my gold chain paid
the bill at the pharmacy.

Your father had vanished.
But the world is small.

A woman with nothing but pride
appeared one day,

poor, broken, unfortunate,
holding a package.

Woman, she said in a husky voice,
I'm not returning your husband,

I don't know where he is.
But here's this dress,

the last bit of luxury
that I kept as a keepsake

from that scandalous day,
that day of great shame.

I did not love him,
love came later.

By that time, he was repelled
and said that he liked me

as I used to be.

I threw myself at his feet,

tried every wile,
scraped my face on the floor,

pulled my hair,
hurled myself into the stream,

slashed myself with a penknife,
threw myself into the sewer,

drank down faith and gasoline,
prayed two hundred novenas,

woman, it was useless,
your husband has vanished.

I bring you the clothes
that record my wrongdoing

of hurting a wife,
of trampling her pride.

Please take this dress
and give me your pardon.

I looked at her face,
where were those eyes,

that gracious smile,
that neck of camelia,

that waistline
so comely and slim,

those delicate feet
in satin sandals?

I looked at her hard,
without saying a word.

I took the dress,
and hung it on that nail.

And she stole quickly away
while down the street

your father appeared.
He looked silently at me,

hardly noticed the dress
and said only: Woman,

lay my dish on the table.
I did, he sat down,

he ate, wiped his sweat,
he was always the same,

he ate half sideways
and had not aged.

The sound of food
in his mouth warmed me,

gave me great peace,
an exquisite feeling

that all was a dream,
no dress . . . no nothing.

Children, listen! I hear
your father climbing the stairs.
M. S.

# THE ELEPHANT

I make an elephant
from the little
I have. Wood
from old furniture
holds him up, and I fill him
with cotton, silk,
and sweetness.
Glue keeps his heavy
ears in place.
His rolled-up trunk
is the happiest part
of his architecture.
And his tusks are made
of that rare material
I cannot fake.
A white fortune
rolling around
in circus dust
without being
lost or stolen.
And finally there are
the eyes where the most
fluid and permanent
part of the elephant
stays, free of dishonesty.

Here's my poor elephant
ready to leave
to find friends
in a tired world
that no longer believes
in animals and doesn't
trust in things.

Here he is: an imposing
and fragile hulk,
who shakes his head
and moves slowly,
his hide stitched
with cloth flowers
and clouds—allusions
to a more poetic world
where love reassembles
the natural forms.

My elephant goes
down a crowded street,
but nobody looks
not even to laugh
at his tail that threatens
to leave him.
He is all grace, except
his legs don't help
and his swollen belly
will collapse
at the slightest touch.
He expresses
with elegance
his minimal life
and no one in town
is willing to take
to himself
from that tender body
the fugitive image,
the clumsy walk.

Easily moved,
he yearns for
sad situations,
unhappy people,
moonlit encounters
in the deepest ocean,
under the roots of trees,
in the bosom of shells;

he yearns for lights
that don't blind
yet shine through
the thickest trunks.
He walks the battlefield
without crushing plants,
searching for places,
secrets, stories
untold in any book,
whose style only the wind,
the leaves, the ant
recognize, but men
ignore since they dare
show themselves only
under a veiled peace
and to closed eyes.

And now late at night
my elephant returns,
but returns tired out,
his shaky legs
break down in the dust.
He didn't find
what he wanted,
what we wanted,
I and my elephant,
in whom I love
to disguise myself.
Tired of searching,
his huge machinery
collapses like paper.
The paste gives way
and all his contents,
forgiveness, sweetness,
feathers, cotton,
burst out on the rug,
like a myth torn apart.
Tomorrow I begin again.
M. S.

# DEATH IN A PLANE

I awaken for death.
I shave, dress, put on my shoes.
It is my last day: a day
not broken by one premonition.
Everything happens as usual.
I head for the street. I am going to die.

I shall not die now. A whole day
unfolds before me.
What a long day it is! And in the street
what a lot of steps I take! And what a lot of things
have accumulated in time! Without paying much
        attention
I keep on going. So many faces
crowded into a notebook!

I visit the bank. What good
is the money, if a few hours later
the police come and take it
from the hole that was my chest?
But I don't see myself wounded and bloody.
I am clean, spotless, bright, summery.
Nevertheless, I walk toward death.
I walk into offices, into mirrors
into hands that are offered, into eyes
that are nearsighted, into mouths that smile
        or simply talk.
I do not say goodbye, I know nothing, I am
        not afraid:
death hides
its breath and its strategy.

I lunch. What for? I eat a fish in a sauce of
        gold and cream.
It is my last fish on my last
fork. The mouth distinguishes, chooses, decides,
swallows. Music passes through the sweets, a
        shiver
from a violin or the wind, I don't know. It
        isn't death.
It is the sun. The crowded trolleys. Work.
I am in a great city and I am a man
in a cogwheel. I am in a rush. I am going to die.
I ask the slow ones to clear a path for me. I
        don't look
at the cafes rattling with coffee cups and conver-
        sation.
I don't look at the shaded wall of the old
        hospital.
Nor at the posters. I am in a rush. I buy a
        paper. It's a rush
even if it means death!


The day already come around to its midpoint
        does not tell me
that I too have begun to come to an end. I
        am tired.
I want to sleep, but the preparations. The
        telephone.
The bills. The letters. I do a thousand things
that will create another thousand, here, there,
        in the United States.
I'll do anything. I make dates
that I shall never keep, I utter words in vain
I lie, saying: "Until tomorrow." But tomorrow
        won't be.


I decline with the afternoon, my head aches,
        I defend myself,
hand myself a pill: at least
the water drowns what hurts,

the fly, the buzzing . . . but nothing I will
        die from: death cheats,
cheats like a soccer player,
chooses like a cashier,
carefully, among illnesses and disasters.

Still it isn't death, it is the shadow
over tired buildings, the interval between
two races. Heavy business slows down,
engineers, executives, laborers, are finishing up.
But cabdrivers, waiters, and a thousand other
nighttime workers are getting started. The city
changes hands.

I go home. Again I clean up.
So my hair will be neat
and my nails not bring to mind the rebellious
        child of long ago.
The clothes without dust. The plastic suitcase.
I lock up my room. I lock up my life.
The elevator locks me up. I am calm.

For the last time I look at the city.
I can still turn back, put off death,
not take that car. Not go.
I can turn and say: "Friends,
I forgot a paper, there's no trip."
Then go to the casino, read a book.

But I take the car. I point out the place
where something is waiting. The field. Searchlights.
I pass by marble, glass, chrome.
I climb some steps. I bend. I enter
death's interior.

Death arranges seats to make the wait
more comfortable. Here one meets
those who are going to die and do not know it.
Newspapers, coffee, chewing gum, cotton
        for the ear,

small services daintily surround
our strapped-in bodies.
We are going to die, it is not only
my single and limited death,
twenty of us will be destroyed,
twenty of us will die,
twenty of us will be smashed to bits, and right
        now.

Or almost now. First the private,
personal, silent death of the individual.
I die secretly and without pain,
to live only as a piece of twenty,
and in me incorporate all the pieces
of those who are silently dying as I am.
All of us are one in twenty, a bouquet
of vigorous breaths about to be blown apart.

And we hang,
coldly we hang over the loves
and business of the country.
Toy streets disappear,
lights dim, hills dissolve,
there is only a mattress of clouds,
only a cold oxygen tube grazes my ears,
a tube that is sealed: and inside
the illumined and lukewarm body we live
in comfort and solitude, quiet and nothingness.

So smooth in the night is this machine and so
        easily does it cut
through increasingly larger blocks of air
that I live
my final moment and it's as if
I had been living for years
before and after today
a continuous and indomitable life
where there were no pauses, lapses, dreams.

I am twenty in the machine

that purrs softly
between starry pictures and the remote breaths
    of earth,
I feel at home thousands of meters high,
neither bird, nor myth,
I take stock of my powers,
and I fly without mystery,
a body flying, holding onto pockets, watches, nails,
tied to the earth by memory and muscular habit,
flesh soon to explode.

Oh, whiteness, serenity under the violence
of death without previous notice,
careful despite the unavoidable closeness
of atmospheric danger,
a shattering blast of air, splinter of wind
on the neck, lightning
flash burst crack
broken we tumble
straight down I fall and am turned into news.

M. S.

# FAMILY PORTRAIT

Yes, this family portrait
is a little dusty.
The father's face doesn't show
how much money he earned.

The uncles' hands don't reveal
the voyages both of them made.
The grandmother's smoothed and yellowed;
she's forgotten the monarchy.

The children, how they've changed.
Peter's face is tranquil,
that wore the best dreams.
And John's no longer a liar.

The garden's become fantastic.
The flowers are gray badges.
And the sand, beneath dead feet,
is an ocean of fog.

In the semicircle of armchairs
a certain movement is noticed.
The children are changing places,
but noiselessly! it's a picture.

Twenty years is a long time.
It can form any image.
If one face starts to wither,
another presents itself, smiling.

All these seated strangers,
my relations? I don't believe it.

They're guests amusing themselves
in a rarely-opened parlor.

Family features remain
lost in the play of bodies.
But there's enough to suggest
that a body is full of surprises.

The frame of this family portrait
holds its personages in vain.
They're there voluntarily,
they'd know how—if need be—to fly.

They could refine themselves
in the room's chiaroscuro,
live inside the furniture
or the pockets of old waistcoats.

The house has many drawers,
papers, long staircases.
When matter becomes annoyed,
who knows the malice of things?

The portrait does not reply,
it stares; in my dusty eyes
it contemplates itself.
The living and dead relations

multiply in the glass.
I don't distinguish those
that went away from those
that stay. I only perceive
the strange idea of family

travelling through the flesh.

E. B.

# INTERPRETATION OF DECEMBER

Maybe it's the child
suspended in memory.
Two lit candles
in the depths of the room.
And the Jewish face
in the print, maybe.
The smell of various burners
under each pot.
Holy feet walking
in snow, in the backlands,
in the imagination.

The doll broken
before it was played with,
also a wheel
in the garden somewhere,
and the iron train
passing over me
so lightly: It doesn't crush me,
but remembers me instead.

It is the letter written
with difficult letters,
mailed at a post office
without stamp or approval.
The open window
where wandering eyes
lean out,
eyes that ask
and don't know how to give.

The old man sleeping
in the wrong chair.

The torn newspaper.
The dog pointing.
The cockroach scurrying.
The smell of cake.
The wind blowing.
And the clock stopped.

More litany of the mass
than can be suppressed,
the white dress
in a white street
flying back to the cold.
The hidden sweetness,
the forbidden book,
the frustrated bath,
the failed victory,
the dream of dancing
over a floor of water
or that voyage upon
the vastness of time
where the oldest laws
are never reached.

It is loneliness
in front of the chestnut trees,
the dull zone
in the sphere of sound,
the wine stain
in the drunken towel,
displeasure of five hundred
mouths swallowing
false candy
still moist
from the weeping of streets.

The empty hut
in the land without music.
The shared silence
in the land of ants.
The sleep of lizards

that never hear the bell.
Talk of fish
about things liquid.
Stories of the spider
at war with mosquitoes.
Stains of cut
and rotten wood.
Stinginess of stone
in a dull monologue.
The mine of mica
and the figurehead.
The natural night
without enchantment.
Something irreducible
in the life-giving legends
yet incorporated
in the heart of myth.

It is the child within us
or outside us
harvesting myth.
M. S.

# MORNING STREET

The splashing rain
unearthed my father.
I never imagined
him buried thus,
to the din of trolleys
on an asphalt street
giant palm trees slanting on the beach
(and a voice from sleep
to stroke my hair),
as melodies wash up
with lost money                              •
discarded confessions
old papers, glasses, pearls.

To see him exposed
to the damp, acrid air
that drifts in with the tide
and cuts your breath,
to want to love him
without deceit
to cover him with kisses, with flowers, with swallows,
to alter time
to offer the warmth
of a quiet embrace
from this elderly recluse,
discarded confessions
and a lamblike truce.

To feel the lack
of inborn strengths
to want to carry him
to the older sofa
of a bygone ranch,

but splashes of rain
but sheets of mud beneath reddish streetlamps
but all that exists
of morning and wind
between one nature and another,
yawning sheds by the docks
discarded confessions
ingratitude.

What should a man do
at dawn
(a taste of defeat
in his mouth, in the air)
or at any moment
in whatever place?
Everything spoken, drunk, or even pretended
and the rest still buried
in the folds of sleep,
cigarette stubs
the wet glare of streets
discarded confessions
morning defeat.

Vague mountains
greening waves
newspapers already white,
hesitant melody
trying to spawn
conditions for hope
on this gray day, of a broken lament.
Nothing left to remind me
of the seamless asphalt.
Abandoned cellars
my body shivers
discarded confessions:
abruptly, the walk home.

T. C.

81

# INDICATIONS

Perhaps a keener sensitivity to the cold
an inclination to get home earlier
that hesitation before opening the long-awaited
package of books delivered in the mail.
Wondering, shall I go to a movie?
From the three possibilities of your night, you choose none.
Perhaps that look, more serious though not burning,
you sometimes turn upon things, and they comprehend.

Or at least you imagine so. How faithful they are, the things
in your study. The old pen you refuse to exchange
for some other containing the latest chemical secret, an immortal ink.
Those marks on your desk—it's hard to tell whether time,
the wood itself, or the dust engendered them.
You know it well, that desk. Letters, essays, poems
all issued from it, from you. From that hard substance
from its serenity, from that felled forest they came:
the words you unearthed and pieced together, one beside the other.

You run a hand
over its gnarled surface. The varnish worn off. No, the tree
reemerging. The road returning. Itabira in the distance
watching for your arrival, long-expected, without a sound.
The desk grows lighter, as with it you drift
through latitudes of patience, acceptance, resignation.
Watch the desk as it flies! Don't touch it! That winged desk
from whose drawers spring dark pages—secrets, finally liberated
and scattering across the mineral landscape, enshrouded with silence.

Back again, precise familial
territory without dreams. As if already intuiting
that someday these rooms will be emptied, the walls wiped clean
a truck parked outside, and the movers climbing in

while in some municipal registry an entry will be canceled,
you scrutinize intently every scratch,
each color, each facet
of the old familiar things.
The family is, after all, an arrangement of possessions, a sum
of lines, volumes, surfaces. It's the doors,
keys, plates, beds, forgotten parcels,
even corridors, and that space
between the cupboard and the wall
where a certain amount of silence, dust, and silverfish always gathers
and from time to time is swept away . . . but still persists.

By now the explanations are gone. It would be difficult
to comprehend, even this late in time, why one gesture
unfolded, another failed, so many others barely outlined;
as it would be impossible to hold all those voices
overheard at lunch, at dinner, in the interval of night
one year, then another, and on and on and on,
all the voices heard at home in those fifteen years.
Yet they have to be somewhere: congregating,
saturating stairs, leaking from the pipes,
embodying old papers; having lost their strength, their fervor;
existing now only in the cellars of memory.

How can one know? At first it seems deserted
as if nothing remained or a river swelled
through the rooms, submerging all.
The sheets turn yellow, ties fray,
your beard grows in, falls out, teeth loosen,
arms hang limp
particles of food drop from a shaky fork
things keep falling and falling
and yet the floor is clean and smooth.
People start taking to their beds, float in the air, disappear
and everything is smooth, except for the face
bent over the desk, where everything is still.
T. C.

# SONG FOR THAT MAN OF THE PEOPLE
## CHARLIE CHAPLIN

I

It had to be some poet from Brazil
not one of the greatest, more likely to make a fool of himself
shuffling around somewhere in your vicinity or aspiring to dwell
     there
as in the domain, poetic and essential, of lucid dreams

it had to be this obstinate little minstrel
of elementary rhythms, fresh from a small town in the interior
where they don't insist on your wearing a tie but everyone's
     extremely polished
and oppression is abhorred even though heroism's suffused with a
     certain irony

it had to be some long-ago boy of twenty
drawn to your pantomime by threads of tenderness and laughter,
     broken in time,
who would finally venture back, much older now, and pay you a visit
to say a few things to you under the pretext of a poem.

To tell you how we Brazilians have loved you
and that in this, as in everything else, our people are similar
to any other in the world—including the small Jews
with walking stick and derby hat, pointy shoes, melancholy eyes

vagabonds whom the world has expelled, and yet they go on living
     and clowning
on film, along those crooked streets with signboards: Factory, Barber,
     Police,
foiling hunger, dodging brutality, perpetuating love
like a secret whispered into the ear of a common man fallen in the
     street.

I know that no speech, however lullingly bourgeois, is going to affect
     you
that you habitually sleep through the vehement inauguration of
     statues,
that out of so many words surging like traffic through the busy
     streets
only the humblest, a curse or a kiss, can touch you.

It's no greeting of devotees I offer you, of ardent fans
who don't exist, but one from ordinary people in an ordinary town
and I've no pretenses now concerning the substance of this song
     about you
like some airmailed bouquet of absurd flowers addressed to the
     inventor of gardens.

Through me would speak those forever reviled for their unhappiness
     and wildly disgusted with it all

who filed into the theaters like an infestation of rats fleeing life
for the sake of two hours of anesthesia—to hear the music on the
     piano or
commune with images in the darkness—and suddenly they
     discovered you, and were saved.

Through me would speak those forsaken by justice, losers and
     pariahs,
bankrupt, mutilated, deficient, solitary, repressed,
dreamy, indecisive, tender, hopelessly sentimental,
irresponsibly childish, simple of heart, insane, pathetic.

And through me, the flowers you loved so much once stepped upon
through me, the stumps of candles you ate in your quintessential
     poverty,
instruments of your trade, the thousand and one things apparently
     stuck,
each gadget, each object out of the attic, the more obscure they were
     the more they would speak.

Your clothes are suffused with night.
Your dappled vest makes no difference
nor the frozen, formal dress shirt
for an impossible ball without orchids.
You're condemned to black. Your trousers
blend into darkness. Your shoes
bulbous in the dim glare of an alley
are nocturnal toadstools. The quasi-
top hat—black sun—looms raylessly above it all.
Thus, nocturnal citizen of a republic
in mourning, you materialize before our
dubious eyes, which inspect you and reflect:
Behold the gloomy one, the widower, the inconsolable
the raven, the nevermore, the too-late arrival
in a very old world.

And the moon alights
on your face. White, chalked with death,
what sepulchers it evokes or what chilling
submarine stalks, and mirrors
and lilies that some tyrant has severed, and visages
shrouded in flour. The black mustache
sits on you like a warning
but all at once interrupted. It's short, thick
ebony. Oh, white face of lunar landscape
semblance cut from a sheet, tracing on a wall
childhood notebook, scarcely image at all.
Yet the eyes are profound, the mouth from somewhere faraway
knowledgeable, alone, quietly it comes
to smile, a dawn for all.

And now we no longer fear the night.
Death avoids us, we grow smaller
as if, by the touch of your magical cane, restored
to the secret land where all children sleep.
Now it's no longer the office with thousands of files
the garage, the university, the alarm clock
it's the old demolished street with its crowded shops

and off we go with you to smash a windowpane
and off we go with you to topple constables to the ground
and off we go to rediscover in the human anatomy
that place—careful!—that calls for swift kicks: verdict
from a justice far lower than official.


# III

Full of nutritious hypotheses, you stamp out the hunger
of those not invited to our suppers, celestial or
industrial. There are dog bones, puddings made
of jelly and cherry and chocolate and clouds
in all the folds of your overcoat. They've been saved
for the child or the mongrel, since well you know
the need to eat, the smell of soup,
the taste of meat, the white softness of potatoes,
and well you've practiced the subtle art of transforming the humble lace
of your shoes into macaroni.
Well, somehow you've managed dinner again: Life is good!
And now for a smoke, as you lift a cigarette out
from a sardine tin.

There aren't many dinners in the world, you appreciate that,
and the most succulent chickens
on china platters are protected by heavy glass.
There's always a lid, and it never breaks
plus steel, asbestos, the law
an entire army to guard every chicken
while a hunger comes all the way from Canada, and a wind
a glacial voice, a wintry gust, until a leaf
dances indecisively, then lights on your shoulder, faint message
you barely decipher. The inviolable crystal lies somewhere
between chicken and hunger; and between hunger and hand
the law of walls, of distance. So finally you transform yourself
into the great roast chicken that flutters
above all hungers, high in the air: chicken of gold
on paper embers; meal for all
on a day for all, too late to arrive.

# IV

The New Year itself is late, much like your sweetheart.
At the lonely little table your talents are accentuated:
you're a ballet dancer, fluid and incorporeal,
but no one's going to show up and see how you ache
with the ardor of diamonds and the delicacy of dawn
or how the shack, at your touch, turns into the moon.
World of snow and salt, of hoarse gramophones
howling in the distance with pleasures you never partake in.
Inaccessible world, that deprives you of your sweetheart
and every other desire, in the night, for communion.
Your palace evaporates, sleep engulfs you
nobody wanted you, everybody has someone else
you hoped to give all, they wouldn't accept.

Then you step on the ice and slip on a scream.
Yet you've no envy of banquets, nor pride
nor pain nor rage nor malice.
You're the New Year itself, still dawdling along the way. A whole house
        goes
whirling by you, glasses fly
bodies suddenly upturned, and your sweetheart
searching everywhere in the night . . . fails to find you
little you
simple you, ordinary you.

To be so alone in the midst of so many shoulders,
to parade like thousands, in that skinny little body
and have arms big enough to wrap around houses
with your one foot in Guerrero and the other in Texas
to speak the same to a Chinaman as to an Amazonian
a Russian, a black: to become the one and only, among us all
without words, or filters
or opals
that vast city within you, unknown to us.

# V

A blind woman falls in love with you. Suddenly her eyes
open. No, she no longer loves you. A wealthy fellow
befriends you while drunk, but sobered up scorns
your riches. The confusion is ours, as we forget
what there is of water, of breeze, of innocence
at the bottom of each one of us, earthbound as we are.
But oh, the false myths we abide by: drab flowers
treacherous angels, circular coffers, asthmatically
poetic academies; conventions in blue
white and purple; machinery, piles
of telegrams, factories and factories
and factories of lamps, prohibitions, dawns.
You're just a common laborer
ordered about by the angry voice through the megaphone.
You're a cog, a spasm, a grimace.
I pick up your parts, still vibrating,
mutilated lizard.

I paste your pieces together. Yours
is a strange oneness, in a world completely pulverized.
And we, who at each step cover
and undress and mask ourselves,
scarcely grasp the same man in you
               apprentice
               fireman
               cashier
               confectioner
               emigrant
               convict
               mechanic
               groom
               skater
               soldier
               musician
               wayfarer
               circus performer
               marquis
               sailor

                    piano mover
meanwhile always only you yourself
the one who doesn't agree but is too meek,
incapable of ownership, foot-
loose, an open road, the friend
we'd like to come in
out of the rain, the mirror, the memory,
and still we lose him.


## VI


I no longer think of you, but only of the trade
you practice. Strange watchmaker,
you sniff at the dismantled parts and the mainspring
activates: time commences. You're a window washer.
You sweep streets. It doesn't matter
if the urge to shirk eats away at you. And the next corner
makes another man of you, while logic
excludes from you its calculating privileges.

Oh, there's energy in you, but capricious
but benevolent
and from it emerge arts in no way bourgeois
products of thin air and tears, apparel
which presents us with wings or petals, and trains
and ships without steel, where our friends
by spinning in place can travel through time
where books become animated, paintings talk
and everything set free dissolves
into an effusion of love without recompense, and smiles, and sunshine.

Your trade, it's one that places you
right in the midst of us all:
vagabond between two shifts, a skilled hand
at hammering, cutting, threading, plastering,
your feet insist on shuffling you round the world.
Your hands poke about for some implement: it's a razor
and to the rhythm of Brahms you commence to shave
in that forgotten barbershop at the heart of an oppressed world
where after so much emptiness and silence we repossess you.

You were right to have kept quiet.
You pondered in the shadow of locks
chains, striped clothes, barbwire fences
you piled up harsh words, stones, cement, bombs, accusations
you registered with a hidden pencil the thousands of deaths, the
    thousands
of bleeding mouths, the thousands of arms enfolded.
You said nothing at all. But a lump, a gorge
forming, and the words about to spew.
Oh, demoralized words, rescued finally, spoken anew.
Oh, power of human expression inventing new words and breathing
    fresh life into the old, long exhausted.
Oh, dignity of the voice sounded in just anger and profound love,
root of the human spirit, irritated tree, withstanding the fury and
    oppression of dictators.
Oh, Charlie, mine and everyone's companion, your shoes and
    mustache amble along a highway of dusty hope.

T. C.

# from NOVOS POEMAS

## (New Poems)
### 1947

# THE DISAPPEARANCE OF LUISA PORTO

## 1

Ask anyone who knows
the whereabouts of Luisa Porto
to please notify her residence
at 48 Santos Oleos Street.
Immediately advise
her poor sick mother
for many years a cripple
now beside herself with grief.

If you happen to come across
Luisa Porto, age 37, make her
come home, get her to write
or send word where she is.
Ask some amateur reporter
a passing stranger, salesclerk, exterminator
anybody at all, from whatever class
even the well-to-do,
to have pity on a worried mother
and bring back her daughter
or at least some news.
Luisa's tall, thin
dark hair, downy complexion, white teeth
a beauty mark by her left eye
rather nearsighted
plainly dressed, glasses.
Disappeared three months ago.
A sickly mother's appeal.

Call upon the charitable people in our city
to assist in a family matter
worthy of special concern.

Luisa's a good girl, affectionate
religious, hardworking, proper.
She left to do some shopping at the corner market
and never came back.

She had so little money in her pocket.
(Find Luisa.)
She's not the type to come home late.
(Find Luisa.)
She didn't have any boyfriend.
(Find her, find her.)
It's unbearable without her.

## 2

If in the meantime you can't find her,
don't just give up looking;
with persistence and faith, God will reward you,
you're bound to spot her sooner or later.
Her mother, a poor widow, never loses hope;
remember that Luisa seldom went downtown
so it's best to start right here in the neighborhood
her closest friend (not counting her mother)
is the seamstress Rita Santana, a frivolous girl
who apparently can shed no light on the matter
and limits herself to repeating: I don't know, I don't know!
which, to say the least, is odd.

So many people disappear, year after year,
in a city like Rio
Luisa Porto may never be found.
Once, in 1898
or 9,
the chief of police vanished from sight
after stepping out one night to have a look around Rossio Square
and till this very day . . .
Luisa's mother, at the time a young girl,
read it in the *Merchants Daily*
and was astonished
the headline printed across her memory.

How could she have guessed that a brief marriage, then widowhood
poverty, paralysis, and regret
would prove her lot in life;
that her only daughter, as sweet as she was nearsighted,
would vanish without explanation.

For the last time, and in the name of God
all-powerful in His goodness and mercy
find the poor girl, the one
called Luisa Porto
the one without a boyfriend.
Forget politics for a moment
set aside materialistic concerns
and devote some time to searching
making inquiries, nosing around.
You won't regret it. There's no
satisfaction greater than the smile
of a joyous mother
or the inner peace
that comes from simple acts of charity
pure ablution to the soul.

### 3

Don't try to tell me that Luisa committed suicide.
The holy fire of faith
burned within her soul
devoted to God and the Blessed Mother of our little Lord Jesus.
She would never take her life.
You've got to find her.
She could hardly be the victim of a disaster
if the police know nothing
and the press is uninformed.
The child lives for the consolation of her crippled mother
bearing witness to the absolute triumph of maternal love
Christian piety
filial duty.

And no insinuations regarding her virtue:
She did not, I repeat, did not have a boyfriend.

Something extraordinary will turn out to have happened:
an earthquake or the advent of a king;
the streets must have changed directions
for her to take so long; it's dark!
But I know she'll come back, either by herself
or led by a generous hand,
looking sheepish and tender
as a song.

At any hour of the day or night
whoever finds her, please advise Santos Oleos Street.
There's no telephone
only an old housekeeper you can give your message to
and she'll take care of the rest.

But
should you decide that the fate of nations is far more important
that we mustn't waste time on particular griefs;
if you've shut your ears to the ringing of the bell
that's all right, insult Luisa's mother
turn the page:
God will show compassion for the lost, the forsaken
will minister to the lame, whose limbs
will unbend in the form of a quest.
God Himself will say:
Go,
find your only daughter, kiss her, and forever hold her to your
        heart.

4

Or perhaps that heavenly favor won't be needed after all.
Luisa's mother (all of us are sinners)
would feel unworthy of such grace.
And hope remains, which is itself a gift.
Yes, the stray lambs one day return
or never, or maybe, or always.
And by thinking we understand.
All she wants is her child
who on a distant afternoon, back in Cachoeiro,

had just been born and smelled of milk
colic, and tears.
There's no need for more description
or this—forgive me—photograph:
vague shadows of a living being
which hardly tell you anything.
No more searching. Silence the radios.
The calm of petals opening
in a blue garden
where hearts are unburdened, and the figure of a virgin
untouched for all time.
And through feeling we comprehend.
There's no use looking any longer
for my dear daughter Luisa, who
—while I wander through the ashes of the world
with these useless limbs affixed to me, while I suffer
and by suffering I release and reconcile myself
and return to life, and walk—
looms motionless
caught in the heart of that invisible star
Love.

т. с.

*from* CLARO
ENIGMA

*(Evident Enigma)*
*1951*

# AN OX LOOKS AT MAN

They are more delicate even than shrubs and they run
and run from one side to the other, always forgetting
something. Surely they lack I don't know what
basic ingredient, though they present themselves
as noble or serious, at times. Oh, terribly serious,
even tragic. Poor things, one would say that they hear
neither the song of air nor the secrets of hay;
likewise they seem not to see what is visible
and common to each of us, in space. And they are sad,
and in the wake of sadness they come to cruelty.
All their expression lives in their eyes—and loses itself
to a simple lowering of lids, to a shadow.
And since there is little of the mountain about them—
nothing in the hair or in the terribly fragile limbs
but coldness and secrecy—it is impossible for them
to settle themselves into forms that are calm, lasting,
and necessary. They have, perhaps, a kind
of melancholy grace (one minute) and with this they allow
themselves to forget the problems and translucent
inner emptiness that make them so poor and so lacking
when it comes to uttering silly and painful sounds: desire, love,
      jealousy
(what do we know?)—sounds that scatter and fall in the field
like troubled stones and burn the herbs and the water,
and after this it is hard to keep chewing away at our truth.
M. S.

# SONG FOR A YOUNG GIRL'S ALBUM

Good morning: I said to the girl
who smiled from far away.
Good morning: but she didn't
respond from the distance.
Eye contact was pointless
so I waved my arms
good morning to the girl who,
day or night,
was far out of my range,
far from my poor good morning.
Good morning forever: maybe
the answer will come cold
or come late, yet
I shall wait
for her good morning.
And over the rows of houses,
over the hills and valleys,
I shall lamely repeat
at whatever hour: good morning.
Maybe the time is wrong
and my sadness too great
to warrant
this absurd good morning.
The girl does not know,
or sense, or suspect
the tenderness within
the heart of my good morning.
Good morning: I repeat
in the afternoon;
at midnight: good morning.
And at dawn
I color my day
blue and pink:

so the girl can find it!
good morning.
Good morning: only an echo
in the bushes (but who can say)
makes out my message
or wishes me good morning.
Smiling from far away,
the girl in her joy
does not feel the violence
in the radiance of this
good morning.
Night that had betrayed
sadness, trouble, confusion,
wanders without fire
in the wildest nostalgia.
If only she would say
good morning to my good morning,
the night would change
to the clearest of days!

M. S.

# DEATH OF THE HOUSES
# IN OURO PRÊTO

Over rooftops, over time
the rain washes. And walls
that had watched men die
seen the gold slip away
known an empire's passing
(mutely comprehended)
crumble now; to die as well.

Set thus on the hillside
less rustic than proud
in their humble whites
blues, pinks, vermilions
how permanent they seemed
and were not! As the rain
thrums on lattice and sill,

the trellis slowly rots
like decomposing lace
from a funeral dress.
Doors fall off their hinges.
Only a monorhythmic rain
seeps down through history
and the night. Houses die,

die austerely, and with time
matter itself comes to tire
of such subservience to man.
Mortar begins to macerate.
In the sierra, how subtly
things return, to and from
themselves—yet lost now!

The ground begins to recover

the foundations laid so
long ago, summoning all
to relapse into earth again:
that wood be reembodied in trees
now rafters! that dust return
to simple dust along the highways!

The rain washing down, in gullies:
how it lashes, how it beats
upon the landscape of memories
how it strikes, how it bruises
how it pierces the marrow
how it stings, how it wounds
with its rain of arrows

in the foothills of Minas
Gerais! Oh my weatherbeaten
houses, my whiplashed walls,
my wainscot of matted straw,
my corbeled eaves, my mansions
of tiled roofs, exposed rafters
—now dank and humbled.

Down they come, in the torrent,
the old venerable houses
(where we made love, gave birth
and buried our treasures
with a drink to ward off the chill)
swept away in the wind, the rubble,
the bats and the hoarfrost.

While still others decay
with an acid pulverulence
until we scarcely register
their extinction. How they die!
How they're left to merely expire!
The peeling paint, the rotting timbers:
how they vanish before our eyes.

Upon the city I focus

this experienced eye
this keen, whetted gaze
of someone versed in the matter
(those I've lost have taught me)
and watch that viscous arrival
hover above the calm.

It's not enough to witness a man's
death, to understand mortality.
A thousand others spring forth
within, around us, on the earth.
Death, the damp falcon, glides
out of the wilderness. Its beak
pocks away at the massive walls

to pulverize a dying Ouro Prêto.
Upon the bridge, upon the rocks
upon the folded Flemish linens
a blanket of mist
(no longer a downpour)
tells me by what mystery
love is bathed in death.
T. C.

# THE TABLE

And you never liked parties . . .
Old man, what a party
we'd give for you today.
The sons that don't drink
and the one that loves to drink,
around the wide table,
gave up their grim diets,
forgot their likes and dislikes;
it was an honest orgy
ending in revelations.
Yes, old man, you'd hear things
to shock your ninety years.
But then we didn't shock you,
because—what with the smiles,
and the fat hen, and the wine,
good wine from Portugal,
as well as what was made
from a thousand ingredients
and served up in abundance
in a thousand china dishes
—we'd implied already
that it was all in fun.
Yes. Your tired eyes
used to reading the country
in distances of leagues,
and in the distance one steer
lost in the blue blue,
looked into our very souls
and saw their rotten mud,
and sadly stared right through us
and fiercely swore at us
and sweetly pardoned us

(pardon is the usual ritual
for parents, as for lovers).
And then, forgiving all,
you inwardly congratulated
yourself upon such children . . .
Well, the biggest scoundrels
have turned out a lot better
than I bargained for. Besides,
chips off the old . . . You stopped,
frowning suddenly,
inwardly going over
some regretted memory,
and not all that remote,
smiling to yourself, seeing
that you had thrown a bridge
from the grandfather's crazy dance
to the grandsons' escapades,
knowing that all flesh
aspires to degradation,
but on a fiery road
beneath a sexual rainbow,
you coughed. *Harrumph.* Children,
don't be silly. Children?
Great boys in our fifties,
bald, who've been around,
but keeping in our breasts
that young boy's innocence,
that running off to the woods,
that forbidden craving,
and the very simple desire
to ask our mother to mend
more than just our shirts,
our impotent, ragged souls . . .
Ah, it would be a big
*mineiro*\* dinner . . . We ate,
and hunger grows with eating,
and food was just a pretext.
We didn't even need

*\*Referring to the State of Minas Gerais.*

to have appetites; everything
was disposed of; the morning after,
we'd take the consequences.
Never disdain *tutu.* *
There goes some more crackling.
As for the turkey? *Farofa* †
needs a nice little *cachaça* ‡
to keep it company,
and don't overlook the beer,
a great companion, too.
The other day . . . Does eating
hold such significance
that the bottom of the dish
alone reveals the best,
most human, of our beings?
Is drinking then so sacred
that only drunk my brother
can explain his resentment
and offer me his hand?
To eat, to drink: what food
more fragrant, more mysterious
than this Portuguese-Arabian,
and what drink is more holy
than this that joins together
such a gluttonous brotherhood,
big-mouths, good fellows all!
And the sister's there who went
before the others, and was
a rose by name, and born
on a day just like today
in order to grace your birthday.
Her name tastes of camelia
and being a rose-amelia,
a much more delicate flower
than any of the rose-roses,
she lived longer than the name,
although she hid, in secret,

*Dish made of beans mixed with manioc flour.
†Dish made of manioc flour mixed with butter, sausage, eggs, etc.
‡Fiery liquor made from sugarcane.

the scattered rose. Beside you,
see: it has bloomed again.
The oldest sat down here.
A quiet, crafty type
who wouldn't make a priest,
but liked low love-affairs:
and time has made of him
what it makes of anyone;
and, without being you,
strangely, the older he grows,
the more he looks like you,
so that if I glimpse him
unexpectedly now
it is you who reappear
in another man of sixty.
This one has a degree,
the diploma of the family,
but his more learned letters
are the writings in the blood
and on the bark of trees.
He knows the names of wildflowers
and remembers those of the rarest
fruits of cross-breeding.
Nostalgia lives in him,
a countryfied city-man,
a scholarly country-man.
He's become a patriarch.
And then you see one who
inherited your hard will
and your hard stoicism.
But he didn't want to repeat you.
He thought it not worth the trouble
to reproduce on the earth
what the earth will swallow up.
He loved. He loves. And will love.
But he doesn't want his love
to be a prison for two,
a contract, between yawns,
and four feet in bedroom slippers.
Passionate at first meeting,

dry, the second time,
agreeable, the third,
one might say he's afraid
of being fatally human.
One might say that he rages,
but that sweetness transcends his rage,
and that his clever, difficult
recourses for fooling himself
about himself exert
a force without a name
unless, perhaps, it's kindness.
One kept quiet, not wanting
to carry on the colloquy,
rustling, subterranean,
of the more talkative ones
with new words of her own.
She kept quiet, you weren't bothered.
If you loved her so much like that,
there's something in her that still
loves you, in the cross-grained way
that suits us. (Not being happy
can explain everything.)
I know, I know how painful
these family occasions are
and to argue at this minute
would be to kill the party
and you—one doesn't die
once, and not forever.
Due to the disagreements
of our blood in the bodies
it runs divided in,
there are always many lives
left to be consumed.
There are always many dead
left to be reincarnated
at length in another dead.
But we are all alive.
And more than alive, joyful.
We are all as we were
before we were, and no one

can say that he didn't get
something from you. For example:
there at the corner of the table,
but not to be humble, perhaps
out of pure vanity
and to show off his awkwardness
in carefully awkward poses,
there you see me. What of it?
Keep calm. Keep calm. I'm working.
After all, the good life
still is only: life
(and neither was it so good,
nor is it so very bad).
Well, that's me. Observe:
I have all the defects
I didn't smoke out in you,
nor do I have those you had,
any more than your qualities.
Never mind: I'm your son
just by being a negative
way of affirming you.
Oh, how we fought and fought!
Wow! It wasn't funny,
but—the paths of love,
only love can track them down.
I gave you such scant pleasure,
none, perhaps . . . unless
I may have given you
a sort of hope of pleasure,
the indifferent satisfaction
of one who feels his son,
just because of being useless,
may turn out to be, at least,
not a bad character.
I'm not a bad character.
If you suspect it, stop;
I'm not any of those things.
Some affections still
can get at my bored heart.
I bore myself? Too much.

That's my trouble. One failing
I didn't inherit from you.
Well, don't keep looking at me,
there are many still to see.
Eight. And all lower-case,
all frustrated. What sadder
flora could we have found
to ornament the table!
But no! Of such remote,
such pure, forgotten ones
on the sucking, transforming earth,
are the angels. How luminous!
Their rays of love shine out,
and among the empty glasses
their glasses clink until
even the shadows reverberate.
They are angels that deign
to participate in the banquet,
to sit on the little stool,
to live a child's life.
They are angels that deign
that a mortal return to God
something of his divine
ethereal, sensitive substance,
if he has, and loses, a child.
Count: fourteen at the table.
Or thirty? Or were there fifty?
How do I know—if more
arrive, daily, one flesh
multiplied and crossed
with other loving flesh?
There are fifty sinners,
if to be born's a sin,
and demonstrate, in sins,
those we were bequeathed.
The procession of your grandsons,
lengthening into great-grandsons,
comes to ask your blessing
and to eat your dinner.
Take notice, for an instant,

of the chin, the look, the gesture,
of the profound conscience,
and of the girlish grace,
and say, if, after all,
there isn't, among my errors,
an unexpected truth.
This is my explanation,
my best or unique verse,
my all, filling my nothing.
And now the table, replete,
is bigger than the house.
We talk with our mouths full,
we call each other names,
we laugh, we split our sides,
we forget the terrible
inhibiting respect,
and all our happiness
blighted in so many black
commemorative banquets
(no use remembering now),
gestures of family affection
accumulated, held back
(no use remembering now),
the kind and gentle words
that said at the right time
could have changed our lives
(no use changing now),
are at table, spreading out
unprecedented food.
Oh, what more celestial supper
and what greater joy on earth!
Who prepared it? What incomparable
vocation for sacrifice
set the table, had the children?
Who was sacrificed? Who paid
the price of all this labor?
Whose was the invisible hand
that traced this arabesque
in flowers around the pudding,
as an aureole is traced?

Who has an aureole? Who
doesn't have one, since
aureoles are gold, and she
wanted to share it quickly,
and with the thought, she did.
Who sits at the left side,
bent over that way? What white,
but what white more than white
target of white hair
draws the color from the oranges,
cancels the coffee, and
outshines the seraphim?
Who is all light and is white?
You had no presentiment
surely, how white can be
a more diverse tinge
of whiteness itself . . . Purity
elaborated in
your absence, and made perfect,
cold, concrete and lunar.
How could our party be
for one and not for two?
Now you are reunited
in a wedding ring much greater
than the simple ring of earth,
together at this table
of wood more lawful* than any
law of the republic.
Now you are above us,
and above this dinner
to which we summoned you
so far—at last—to love you
and loving, delude ourselves
at a table that is

                                empty.

E. B.

*The phrase for hardwood is madeira de lei, lawful wood.

117

*from* A VIDA
PASSADO
A LIMPO

*(Fair Copy of Life)*
*1958*

# TO A HOTEL
## SCHEDULED FOR DEMOLITION

Goodbye, Hotel Avenida.
Your guests await you
on some other horizon.

You were huge and red,
in each room you had
a curious mirror.

In it was reflected
the passage of each figure
and the rest not to be read

even through the cracks
in the door: what one hides,
pulp of self, and shrieks

without making a sound.
And by adding other faces
in continuous succession,

the mirror wore a thousand masks
of Minas Gerais, Rio, and São Pau-
lists: good and bad: faces.

50 image-years
and 50 on folding
bed 50 with trundles

     nocturnal and confident
     humbly preserving for us
     the uric-acid truth.

(But you lived a long time, Hotel, and in your paunch
whatever was noxious would smile in the dust within you.)

The slow and crimson alexandrine decomposed.
Couples coupling together in the whispering
Carioca* smut, streetcars sparksmelling, politicians
politicianing along insipid corridors
Italian starlets, doormen in ecstasy
    elevator
boys in a panic:
how is such voluptuousness to fit itself
into those four flimsy paneled partitions?
Trays go by silverundulating:
Give me some coffee marmalade morning papers I don't care.
The woman was naked in the center of the room and received
me with the appropriate solemnity of traveling deities:
*Stellen Sie es auf den Tisch!*

No, I was not your room servant, not even some
*boy* in your network of communications or a
setting in the daily fuss of prandial service.
Then how is it I'm living out your archives
and feeling cheated really that I never was
in your register the way the dead
are in their numbered compartments?

I act out love affairs I never had
but in you were had pell-mell.
The way the snail
of memories oozes on
        down the stairs
from the two-hundred thousand bodies lodged within you
records recordsds recordsdsds recordsdsdsds
dsdsdsdsdsdsdsdsds
137 is buzzing
hurry the man is dying
is it aspirins? a priest he wants?
No, not if he's a priest himself and is praying
for the sake of the sins of this hotel
and of any other hotel along the road
which man travels from one to another, which at no

*Carioca: Rio de Janeiro.

point has beginning or ending;
and is only the road and always always
is populated with gestures and departures
and arrivals and fleeing and mileage.
He prays he dies and in solitude
a faucet
drips
and the shower
showers
and the blue
flame of gas heater hisses in the bath
above Carioca Square in flower in the sun.

(Through the scaffolding I see you
not broken disemboweled defiled
imagining you unharmed
emerging from the marching sambas of the military police, from
                    the howling chorus of fans on the radio
                    broadcast of the world's championship
offering to one and all, Hotel Avenida,
an unfading victory laurel.)

You were Time itself and you presided
over the fevered recognition of fingers
love without any real place in the city
over collusion of swindlers, over the expectancy
of employment, over stagnation of governments
over the life of the nation in terms of the individual
and over mass movements that came spilling their ways
into the monastic arcade that houses your streetcars.

You were the heart of Brazil,
Carioca nostalgias rocked back and forth
in your lap, diamond buyers came to you
entrusting their stones, cattle drovers
grazed their herds on the terrace
and the sticky sweetness of provincial tears
was packed away each instant in envelopes
(blue ones?) into the management's pigeonholes
and you were a lot of coffee and some promissory notes.

What professor professes the Law of Things
in some illusive alcove, lecturing
to cockroaches too busy to listen?
What flute insists upon playing its sonatina
without piano always after curfew hour?
And the manias of the oldest lodgers
who are visited at night by Chief Prefect Passos to discuss
the latest urban developments?

And your dead guests
incomparably hotel dead defrauded
of that familial death to which we aspire
as if to some kind of not-dead-death;
the dead who must be dispatched
quickly, so as not to contaminate sheets
and cupboards
with that peculiar chilliness which encompasses them
and there must be no memory in this bed
of whatever is not simply life at Avenida.

Hear the litany of intestinal bubbles?

*Balcony of messengers immobile boatmen*
*newsstand news for never and more*
*white laundry rooms with fluted remains*
bonbonnières *where silver wrappings*
*form serenades on feminine lips*
*telephonic switchboard sullenly aphonic*
discothèque *lamentation of slipped discs*
        *stationery shops*
        *conversation corners*
*Brahma beer best brand for a loving man*
*and the Bar Nacional's simple amiability is*
*suddenly resurrecting Mário de Andrade*
        What to do with the clock
        what to do with ourselves
        without time without some point
        without counterpoint without
        a measure of extension
        or even an obituary

while in ashes the
impatient bison flees
whom no one's ever held
by the horns, affliction?
He marks time mar-
king-king-king
and we alone are marked
with all the failures
of repressed loves
clock which I cannot hear
which will not listen
*robot* of simple smell
tracking the immense
country of motionless touch
the directions I ran
at your command now end
in the crossing of a T
in vague nightmares
in dejected shadows
where all of our intentions
somehow became stratified.

There's no destroying you
the way termites chew up
book earth existence.
Your hands, yes, voraciously
they scrape away at
the tunic of Venus
the large hand the small
this tattooed verse
and everything I've done
to elude you and everything
in the arkademies the
autarchic institutions
historic and astute
which is taught with malice
concerning the evolution of things
oh hotel clockkeeper
god of the cautious man from Minas,
        silence.

125

propriety.
But everything you offended
now avenges itself upon you
      deliberately
with the black arts of witchery.
We swallow your windows
stifling the utterance
of splintering glass which
still struggles, throbbing,
for the moment of hope
when in the evening the breeze
of hoping has passed.

*Scream of a child being born.*

*Please, my poet friend Martins Fontes, can you recite your
odes a little lower while my wife finishes giving birth in the
room above, and the poet did softly sing, but when the baby
came into the world it was the father who was dancing poetry
and asking his poet friend to celebrate before all, guests, maids,
and sparrows alike, with uplifting song the gratifying inspiration.*

*Your night would fall. At the crossroads, there down below,
ragpickers, jacks-of-all-trades, lottery vendors sat swallowing their
prizes with a sip of rum.*

Mujer malvada, yo te mataré! *actors rehearsing in their
rooms?* I will grind your bones to dust, and with your blood
and it I'll make a paste.* *A bunch of trash downstairs.*

Every hotel is flow. A current
passes through walls, carrying the man
his emanations of substance. Every hotel
is dead, is born again; passing; if pigeons
stop over in one, they inhabit what is not to be inhabited
but merely severed. Other houses take hold
and let themselves be possessed or try to, awkwardly.
Space attempts to fix itself. Life becomes spatialized,

*English in the original.

models itself on sentimental crystals.
The doors close every blessed night.
You fail to shut yourself, you cannot. Every minute
someone says goodbye to your unfaithful armoires
and the new arrivals already have return tickets in their bags.
*220 Fremdenzimmer* and you see yourself always empty
and the mirror is reflecting another mirror
and the corridor is leading to another corridor
man when naked indefinitely.

In the heart of Rio de Janeiro
    absence
in the cattle stockade of streetcars
    absence
in the procession of Saturdays
in the rubbing and clanking of carnival groups
    absence
in the arias of Palermo
in the wail of evening papers
    absence
worm consuming apple
worm consuming worm
self-consuming worm
worm worms worm

and the anxiety of finish, which has no hope
of that velvet termination of old ruins
or the quick burst of death from hydrogen.

You were Amazonian solitude
getting-to-be home
in getting-to-be city where lizards.
    Come on, old Malta
    snap a picture for me
    pulverashen effigimage
    of this obscure place.

    Add a few kiosks
    turn-of-the-century
    no water nymphs or forests

but pitifully lice-ridden.

For an inscription
ITATIAIA CHEESE
and whatever else spells
a servile condition.

For these halls, so ugly
much more than dirty
are twisted cells
molluscoid conches
of donkey without a tail
ignorantly in bondage
and some poor devil
within, hunger without.

Old Malta, *s'il vous plaît,*
get another shot:
the hotel marquee
bigger than the Rio Apa.

Still not struck there
in your ethereal seat,
Malta, sub-reptitiously,
by that super construction

which looms out of the ground?
Give me your future picture,
since the urgent thing is to

document each successive possession of place up to the final
judgment and even beyond if there is such a thing as three times
three our belief in a supreme bureau of records for fixed prop-
erties going beyond the human instant and the pulverization of
the galaxies.

How is it I remember you so completely when
I never placed a single stone upon stone of you?
But your name—AVENIDA—followed the lead
of my verse and was ampler with more

forms than your accommodations contained
(time degraded them and death saves them),
and where the foundation has fallen and the instant
fled I am compromised forever.

I am compromised forever
I who for so many years have been in and out
the Grand Hotel of the World without manager

in which, nothing concrete existing,
—avenida, avenida—I house
tenaciously the secret guest of me.
T. C.

*from* A PAIXÃO
MEDIDA

*(Passion Measured)*
*1980*

# SUPPOSED EXISTENCE

What is a place like
when no one passes through?
Do things exist unseen?

The inside of the flat where no one lives,
the tweezers left forgotten in a drawer,
the eucalyptus trees at night along
the thrice-deserted road,
the ant beneath the earth on Sunday,
the dead, one minute after burial,
we, all alone,
in the mirrorless room?

What do they do, what are they,
things not testified as things,
minerals not discovered—that someday
will be?

Unthought-of star,
word scratched out on paper
that no one ever read?
Does it, does the world exist
only through the look
that creates it and confers on it
a specialness?

Concreteness of things: fallacy
of deceptive eye, false ear,
hand that jumps to grasp the not
and grasping it concedes it
the illusion of form
and the illusion greater yet of sense?

133

Or is all valid
flatly, in the absence
of our judicial inquiry
and the latter exists but with the consent
of elements inquired into?
Is all perhaps a hypermarket
of possibles and most possible impossibles
that generate my fantasy of consciousness
while I
exercise the lie of strolling,
but I am strolled upon by the stroll
which is the true sum, amusing itself
with this dream-mist of sensing me
and enjoying events of the passage?

Behold the fearful
battle drawn
between invented being
and the inventing world.
I am a fiction in revolt
against the one-sided mind
and I try to build myself
again at every instant, every cramp,
in the task of tracing
my beginning only mine
and sending out an arc of will
to cover the whole deposit
of sovereign things around.

The war without quarter continues
undefined,
made of negation, weapons of doubt,
tactics to be turned against me,
in stubborn interrogation to find out
if the enemy exists, if we exist
or are all a hypothesis
of strife
in the sun of the short day in which we fight.

G. R.

# About the Author

CARLOS DRUMMOND DE ANDRADE, who is universally recognized as the greatest living Brazilian poet, was born on October 31, 1902, in the small mining town of Itabira in the state of Minas Gerais, where his father was a rancher. He studied in a Jesuit school from which he was eventually expelled for "mental insubordination." After marrying, helping to start a Modernist literary journal in Minas Gerais and obtaining a degree in pharmacology, he became a civil servant in the Department of Education. His first book of poems appeared in 1930. In 1934 he moved to Rio de Janeiro where he has lived ever since.